Slug Bread
&
Beheaded Thistles

Amusing & Useful Techniques for

Nontoxic Gardening & Housekeeping

by
Ellen Sandbeck

De la
Terre
Press

De la Terre Press
P.O. Box 16483
Duluth, MN 55816
(218) 727-8524

Slug Bread & Beheaded Thistles: Amusing and Useful Techniques for Nontoxic Gardening and Housekeeping

Printed in the United States of America by Thomson-Shore, Inc.

First printing 1995

95 96 97 98 99   5 4 3 2

The following publishers have generously given permission to use quotations from copyrighted works: "pity the poor spiders" from *archy and mehitabel* by Don Marquis. Used by permission of Doubleday, a division of Bantam, Doubleday, Dell. "Hot Weather" and "A Winter Diary" from *One Man's Meat* by E.B. White. Copyright 1944 by E.B. White. Published by HarperCollins, used by permission. *Toxicology : A Primer* by Michael A. Kamrin. Lewis Publishers 1988, a subsidiary of CRC Press, Boca Raton, Florida. With permission. "Eat Your Carrots," *Shoe* #260,000 by MacNelly. Copyright 1993 by Tribune Media Services. Reprinted by permission of Tribune Media Services.

Text and illustrations: Ellen Sandbeck

ISBN 0-9646164-0-8

Layout and design by Tony Dierckins Publishing Services
218-424-7921

❂ Printed on Recycled paper ❂

This book
is dedicated
to my friend
Susie Newman,
the patron saint of
using everything
more than once.
If more people
were like Susie,
the world would
be a much happier
and healthier place.

CONTENTS

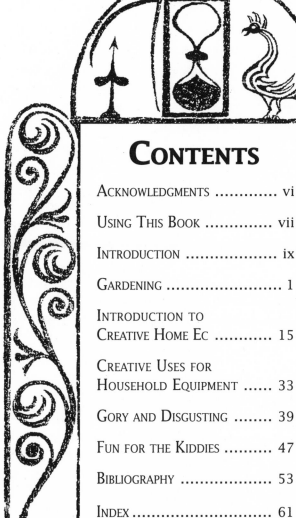

ACKNOWLEDGMENTS

I would like to thank the following people for all their help and support in getting *Slug Bread and Beheaded Thistles* written and published:

My father, Leo J. Berne, who always told me I could accomplish whatever I wanted to in life, and who has been incredibly supportive in many ways.

My husband, Walter, without whom I would grind to a halt.

My cousin Dan King, for his support and the use of his copy machine.

Betsy Damon and the other artist and scientist members of Keepers of the Waters, who got me started on this book.

Jill Jacoby of the Minnesota Pollution Control Agency, for letting me use her computer and teaching me how to use it.

Jim Perlman, of Holy Cow! Press, who has been extremely encouraging and helpful to me in this endeavor, and has walked me through all the steps necessary for self-publishing a book. I would have been completely lost without his help.

The many fine people who read my manuscript for me.

Tony Dierckins, for doing a wonderful layout job.

And last, but certainly not least, the heroic reference librarians of the Duluth Public Library, who go well beyond the call of duty in helping patrons find the information they need. The Duluth Public Library is the best public library I have ever used, and I have used quite a few.

Using This Book

This book is organized with the idea of using and reusing materials as a way to help keep our environment and ourselves healthy. Using things more than once is also a good way to save money.

The sections of the book are organized (if anything that comes out of my mind can be called organized) by materials and methods used to clean houses and eradicate pests. So, for instance, if you have a lot of coffee grounds and you are wondering if there is anything amusing that can be done with them, look up "coffee" in the Index. There you will find various uses for coffee grounds all in one place. If, on the other hand, you want to find a way to remove cigarette smoke from a couch, look up "cigarette smoke, removing" in the index and you will find another use for your old coffee grounds.

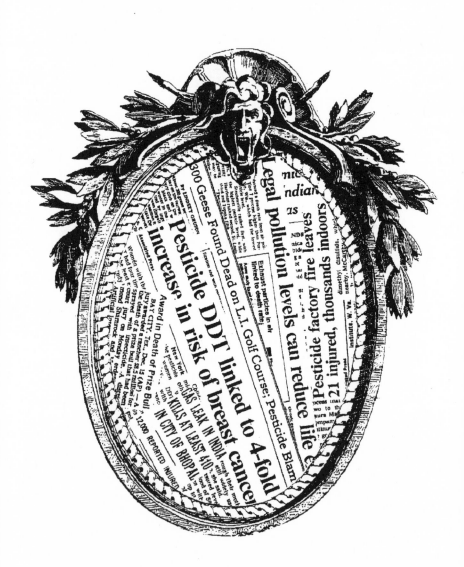

INTRODUCTION

The deadly serious approach to "pest" control has proven to be a deadly mistake. A 1989 report from the World Health Organization/United Nations Environmental Programme estimated that worldwide, over one million human beings are poisoned by pesticides each year; twenty thousand of the poisonings are fatal. Pesticides are the leading cause of work-related deaths in some Latin American countries.

Every year in the U.S., approximately 500,000 tons of pesticides are used, at a cost of $4.1 billion. In an article published in BioScience magazine in 1992, David Pimental, a professor of insect ecology and agricultural sciences at Cornell University, estimated that the annual *indirect costs* of pesticide use in the U.S. are: human pesticide poisonings and related illnesses, $787 million; losses of domestic animals due to pesticide poisonings, $30 million; loss of meat, milk and eggs due to pesticide contamination, $29.6 million; losses due to destruction of natural predators and pollinators: $839.6 million; costs due to pesticide resistance of pest species: $430 million; losses of trees and crops due to excess pesticide contamination: $942 million; monitoring for pesticides and cleaning drinking water: $1.8 billion; destruction of fish and wildlife, $2.2 billion.

Insects are deadly serious, and they are beating us at our own humorless game. Before World War Two only seven species of insects were known to be resistant to chemical pesticides, now over 700 species of plant and animal "pests" are known to be resistant as a result of exposure to pesticides. Despite a tenfold increase in pesticide use in the U.S. since the 1940s, crop losses due to pests have increased by 6%.

In contrast to what is happening to the insects, a 1987 National Cancer Institute study showed that in households where home or garden pesticides are used, children are up

Have pity on the creatures who
dance across your lawn.

to six times more likely to develop leukemia than are children in non-pesticide homes. And, a recent study published in the Journal of the American Medical Association showed that in the U.S. in 1990, deaths due to toxic pollutants and contaminants equaled the number of gunshot and motor vehicle fatalities combined! (There were 60,000 deaths due to environmental pollutants, 35,000 killed by firearms and 25,000 fatalities in motor vehicle accidents.)

We need a new attitude if we are to excel in the human versus pests game; we need to recover our senses of humor and realize that a worm in an apple is not life -threatening, and that nobody ever died of having dandelions in a lawn. We need all the laughs we can get in our dealings with pests, or we will be deadly serious all the way to the cemetery. In 1931, archy the cockroach wrote in his book *archy and mehitabel* (with a little help from his friend, author Don Marquis), *"i will admit that some / of the insects do not lead / noble lives but is every / mans hand to be against them / yours for less justice / and more charity / archy."*

If we do not begin to show more charity towards the earth and her natural systems, the insect, plant and animal "pests" really will inherit the earth; they are a lot tougher than we are. Human beings are an inventive and humorous species; only our sense of humor can save us from the dreadful predicament we have gotten ourselves into. Here is my contribution to the cause: pest control with a giggle (or perhaps it's a smirk).

— Ellen Sandbeck, 1995

". . . To ask for a definite and final answer is to ask to be deceived."

—Michael A. Kamrin, Ph.D.

GARDENING

In 1991, the EPA completed a five-year study entitled "The National Survey of Pesticides in Drinking Water Wells." The study showed that more than half of the 94,000 drinking water wells in the U.S. contained nitrates from fertilizers; 10% of the community wells and 4% of the rural wells contained pesticides. The most commonly detected pesticide was Dacthal, an herbicide used on lawns!

Suburban home owners use more pesticides per acre than farmers do: $1 billion is spent on home pesticides annually at great cost to environmental and human health. Insects and diseases are more likely to attack plants and animals which are weakened through environmental or chemical stress; they stalk the least fit plants in the field or garden, just as predators attack the slowest, weakest members of an animal herd.

Though my husband and I have been landscaping professionally using only organic methods for over a dozen years, I have not had the opportunity to try all of the pest control methods I am including in this chapter.

14.1 million Americans regularly drink pesticide-contaminated water.

We simply have never had many pests to deal with. Having healthy organic soil and choosing only plants that are fully hardy in your climate zone seems to preclude huge infestations of insect pests; and keeping the soil well covered with mulch or ground cover prevents erosion while lowering the weed population. If I have not been able to test them myself, I have tried to be very careful about including only methods that have been well documented.

"Pests" are pests because they are prolific opportunists: human activities are making the world more habitable for pest species, while damaging more delicate organisms.

Variety is the Spice of Life

Plants in a monoculture are more susceptible to insect attack: insects find their food through chemical signals and large groups of a single species create a strong chemical beacon.

The Japanese build bent, crooked garden paths because they believe that evil spirits travel in straight lines. They may be onto something. Insects travel in straight lines —long, straight rows of a single plant species are just what the insect ordered.

"Weeds" are nature's front line defense against bare ground, and they are well-equipped for the job. Some weeds have defensive weapons such as thorns, glue, or poison. Others have amazing reproductive capabilities or brilliant deployment methods: sticky, hitch-hiking seeds (Velcro™ was first invented by burdocks), parachuting seeds, seeds that shoot, seeds that screw themselves into the ground, seeds that digest insects, seeds that can wait like Sleeping Beauty for hundreds of years for the right time to awaken and grow, and plants that spring back to life in greater numbers after being chopped to pieces.

Weeds have to be tough, they have important work to do protecting the earth from devastating erosion. Unfortunately, the important work weeds do goes largely unappreciated by gardeners who have thistles in their rosebeds, dandelions in their lawns, burdock seeds in their dogs' fur, and poison ivy rashes.

LAWNS

The harder we try for the "perfect" single species lawn, the more insect infestations we have, and the weaker the lawn. Lawns are terrific energy wasters in the U.S. In order to keep up with the Joneses, Americans use gas-hogging lawn mowers that emit far more pollution than do cars while cutting the lawns they have just fertilized (with products made of nonrenewable petroleum products) so they will grow faster! The EPA estimates that running a gas mower for one hour generates as much air pollution as running a car for almost two days!

THE PRIMAVERA LAWN CORSET

In order to cut down on your lawn's energy use, as well as air and noise pollution, mow with a push-mower if possible (or at least get an electric mower); plant white Dutch clover in with the grass (clover is a legume which fixes nitrogen in the soil); set the mower to mow as high as possible so weeds get shaded out; leave the grass clippings on the lawn where they can break down and release nutrients into the soil; and when you pull weeds, sprinkle grass and clover seeds in the bare spots.

When you take care of your lawn in an environmentally sound way, you will be rewarded with a thriving earthworm population. Earthworms cannot live in a chemically-contaminated environment, and earthworms are a lawn's best friends. They help keep a lawn well aerated, and each earthworm produces one third of a pound of high quality fertilizer per year! It is a real pleasure watching the early bird hunting worms on your lawn, knowing that it will not become an avian-poisoning victim.

If your lawn is way too big for a push mower and you are not a grounds keeper for a ball team, consider reducing the size of your lawn.

EXORCISING WEEDS

Because weeds evolved to colonize bare soil, fertile soil is relatively weed-resistant. So the first line of defense against weeds is to build up the soil with organic matter. The second

thing to do, especially in perennial beds, is to lay down a thick layer of mulch made of an organic material, (straw, leaves, shredded bark), to prevent weed seeds from reaching the ground.

Lastly, remember that many weed seeds can remain dormant for decades when buried under the ground, and deep tilling can bring these "sleepers" to the surface where they can germinate, producing weeds you may never have seen before. So let sleeping weeds lie, just cover them with a deeper blanket of mulch! If weeds really bother you, try these non-toxic methods for controlling them:

- In the Fall, try blending cabbage leaves in the blender with some water and pouring the resultant mush in the cracks of your sidewalk, in your perennial beds, or anywhere you want to prevent weeds from germinating in the spring.

How does it work? Bernard Bible, a professor at the University of Connecticut, found that cruciferous plants, (cabbage, broccoli, kale, Brussels sprouts etc.), contain thiocyanate, a chemical which is toxic to newly germinated plants, especially those with small seeds. Milder tasting crucifers like cabbage have higher levels of thiocyanate. Brussels sprouts are reported to have the highest levels of thiocyanate, and I am hoping that now I will have a good excuse for not eating them: "I'm sorry, I need to pour these Brussels sprouts in the cracks in my sidewalk, I can't possibly eat them!"

- When injured or killed, winter rye, sorghum, Sudan grass, and winter barley all release chemicals which are toxic to young seedlings. Plant any of these grasses, mow, and use the grass clippings as a weed suppressing mulch.

USING WEEDS

Many weeds are very high in bio-active chemicals which help protect them from insect and animal predation. USDA scientist James A. Duke suggests that the human body may have better tolerance for natural compounds than for man-made compounds: "Man's genes and immune system have been exposed to the natural compounds. They haven't been exposed to tomorrow's synthetic compounds." In fact, one quarter of all prescription drugs contain plant derivatives or synthetic copies of plant compounds.

Battling Poison Ivy and Poison Oak

Poison ivy and poison oak present uniquely difficult problems, and you must be well protected around these plants. When battling your poison ivy, poison sumac, or poison oak patch, always wear appropriate attire—long pants, a long sleeve shirt, hat, goggles, rubber gloves, and rubber boots.

Dig down to expose the plants' roots. Flood the roots with boiling water, then smother the plants with black or clear plastic sheeting, weigh the plastic down on the edges with rocks and dirt, and leave the plastic on all summer. (The boiling water and plastic sheeting method can also be used on other extremely persistent perennial weeds like polygonum or ivy, but you must be diligent about pouring boiling water on any new shoots that come up.)

Never burn any part of a poison oak, sumac, or ivy plant. The smoke disperses the irritating oils very widely and inhaling the smoke can be extremely dangerous.

After you are done with your eradication project, use hot water and detergent to wash all your clothing and to scrub your boots and goggles. Then take a hot shower and scrub yourself thoroughly. If your eradication project seems as if it will take more than a couple of hours, take a shower break every couple of hours to wash the plant oils off your skin. Be careful not to put clothing covered with the plant oils anywhere but in the washing machine! The oils rub off very easily.

In order to keep this small book small, I am including only two examples of my favorite uses for weeds. For more complete information on this extremely interesting and complex subject, please read some of the books on weeds listed in the bibliography. Your local librarian can help you find more information as well.

- **Fatal Attraction**

  Japanese Beetles adore Geranium maculatum, a wild geranium species with small pink flowers. The plant is toxic to Japanese beetles. They are irresistibly attracted to geranium maculatum, eat it, and die!

- **Mustard on the side**

  Mustards and their kin will help clean up salty soils. Plant alyssum in your salty roadside bed, or phlox, or flowering kale, or plain old mustards.

CREATING WEEDS

Some garden plants are like Frankenstein's monster: they turn out to be too rampant to control. The worst weeds in the garden plant category tend to be perennials whose roots travel widely and send up shoots (like Lombardy Poplar and bamboo in warm climates or polygonum in cold climates), plants like ivy which crawl above ground and send down roots, and perennial plants which produce masses of seeds. Chopping up some of these plants only makes them spread more quickly as all the chopped up pieces grow into new plants.

Problems caused by "Frankenstein" plants can affect much more than an individual garden. Purple loosestrife is an escaped garden plant which threatens the balance of wetlands in many parts of the U.S. by crowding out native plants which provide food and shelter for wildlife. Avoid these colonizing pests by consulting experienced gardeners in your area.

His lawn looked just like green velvet!

GOOD WEEDS

"Good weeds" can be created if you plant small annual or perennial plants which reproduce quickly by seeding, but are easy to control. Good examples of these "nice" weeds include alyssum, Johnny-Jump-Ups, Forget-me-nots, poppies, and violets. They are all small, easy to pull out, and pretty. Bear in mind that weeds will colonize every square inch of bare soil in your garden unless the soil is poisoned beyond repair. Wouldn't you prefer to have alyssum growing in the cracks of your sidewalk rather than thistles? How about violets in your lawn instead of plantain? Experienced gardeners in your area should be able to recommend some garden plants that will fit the bill. They will probably even supply you with some!

SOIL CONCERNS

Is your soil a ninety-pound weakling? Build it up!

We lose over 6 billion tons of topsoil annually in the U.S. This is the equivalent of losing 1" of soil off of all the farmland in Maine, New Hampshire, Vermont, New York, New Jersey, Pennsylvania, Delaware, Maryland, Alabama, Arizona, California, and Florida. Human beings cannot survive on a diet of vitamin pills alone, and soil cannot survive on chemicals alone. It is time to start building our soil back up with a healthful diet of manures, mulches, and compost.

FEED YOUR SOIL A HEALTHY DIET—OR PAY THE PRICE!

Inorganic fertilizers cause vegetables to be much higher in nitrates than organically grown vegetables. Remember the scare about nitrosamines in hot dogs causing cancer? Chemically-grown beets, spinach, celery, and lettuce all have higher nitrate levels than do processed meats!

Inorganically-grown produce may not be so good for humans, but it is wonderful for insect pests! Synthetic fertilizers are very high in nitrogen, and all of it tends to be released at once, causing plants to produce overly-tender growth which is irresistible to insect pests. Natural fertilizers act slower.

DON'T DRINK THE WATER...

You don't even have to eat the produce to ingest too many nitrates from fertilizers. Many rural water supplies are heavily contaminated by nitrate-laden runoff from fields; "blue babies" can be one of the effects.

Vast growths, or "blooms" of blue-green algae which can produce deadly toxins, are becoming a worldwide problem, threatening water quality and fisheries. Scientists speculate that the algal blooms are caused by nutrient rich runoff due to deforestation, erosion and over-fertilization.

...AND DON'T BREATHE THE AIR

Increased nitrogen in the soil could be causing a buildup of methane, one of the main "greenhouse" gases, in the atmosphere.

SOIL BUILDING

Many gardening amendments are mined—even some of the organic ones. Mining causes environmental damage, so try to produce your own fertilizers as much as possible. If you buy gardening amendments, try to buy only products made of renewable resources such as manure, crop residues, sea-

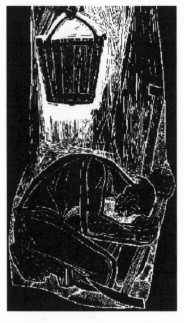

weed, blood meal, bone meal, or shredded wood or bark. For most gardens, however, composting, mulching, bringing home animal manures, and growing green manures should be adequate.

Mulch! Mulch! Mulch!

Mulches discourage diseases and pests and help prevent erosion. Use shredded leaves, dry grass clippings, pine needles, straw, or whatever pesticide-free plant materials you can find and legally bring home. Lake Superior produces a truly wonderful dark, finely shredded mulch made out of driftwood which has been pulverized on its rocks. We bring it home in bags whenever we find piles of it on the shore. When you use mulch, keep the following tips in mind:

- Mulch cool weather crops early in the season to keep the soil cool. Warm weather crops should be mulched after the soil has warmed up.

- Keep mulches away from the trunks of trees and the crowns of perennials to prevent rodent damage and subsequent rot.

- Crushed limestone mulch around trees helps prevent rodents from chewing on tree roots.

- Mulching strawberry plants with sawdust helps prevent slug damage. Use sawdust from untreated wood only.

MANURE

Here is what E.B. White had to say about manure in *One Man's Meat:* "There is no doubt about it, the basic satisfaction in farming is manure, which always suggests that life can be cyclic and chemically perfect and aromatic and continuous."

If you have access to some well composted, chemical-free horse, cow, chicken, or sheep manure, take as much as you can home with you. Use it liberally all over your garden. Do not bother to till it in—if it is left on top of the soil, it will attract earthworms and its nutrients will be more accessible to plants. Make sure you are getting well composted manure; "new" manure may be too "hot" as well as full of viable weed seeds, and uncomposted chicken manure may make you extremely unpopular with your neighbors.

COMPOST

What should you know about compost? Well, for starters:

- Research by Safer Agro-Chem of Victoria, B.C. shows that compost produces fatty acids that are toxic to fungal and bacterial diseases of plants. They found that compost made the passive, low temperature (or "lazy") way was the best at suppressing disease! The lazy way is the best way, something I have long suspected.

- Composting residues from diseased plants may help plants build up immunity to disease. For example, composting clusters of grapes infected with black rot, then using the decomposed material as a mulch around the bases of grapevines helps the vines resist the disease. Mulch "inoculations" against plant diseases work in the same way as vaccinations work for mammals.

- Throw all your leaves, soft clippings, pulled weeds, and vegetable residues in a pile and leave it alone. If your neighbor brags about how hot his compost pile is, explain to him that cool compost has been scientifically proven to be a superior product, then go lounge in a hammock somewhere and listen to a ball game. Plan to use your pile of antibiotic compost next year.

- Soils high in organic matter and nitrogen produce more ethylene than do infertile soils, and ethylene gas discourages the growth of fungus.

- If you are worried about high lead levels in your yard from old paint chips or car exhaust, cover the soil with a huge amount of compost.

How will that reduce lead levels? Research done at Cornell University's Urban Horticultural Institute shows that soils with very high amounts of organic matter in them and a neutral ph (6.5-7) prevent plants from taking up lead and cadmium, even if the lead levels are very high (up to 3,000 p.p.m.). Very well-composted material works better than uncomposted mulch for this purpose.

HELPFUL GARDEN DENIZENS

While being interviewed by the BBC about identifying bugs in the garden, an old English gardener said: "If it moves slowly enough, step on it; if it doesn't, leave it—it'll probably eat something else." Sound advice. What can you do to get insect predators to help you out? Well, for starters:

- Plant the largest variety of plants that you can. Helpful predatory insects like a variety of plants to hide in.

A Little Night Music—Many nocturnal animals will eat garden pests

- Ladybugs and their larvae are the best natural controls of aphids. Ladybugs can be bought by mail-order, but it is sometimes difficult to convince them to stay where you want them. Ladybugs and other insect predators can be encouraged by planting tall flowers and flowering herbs like dill and cilantro in a border around your garden—the predatory insects like to hide in these plants.

- Toads and garden snakes are extremely helpful predators which eat slugs, snails, insects, and even mice. An available source of water such as a small pond or a shallow pan set into the ground will encourage toads and snakes, as will brushy places to hide.

- Bats are the most important predators of night flying insects. Since many of the insects which prey on gardens and gardeners are night flying insects, bats are some of the gardener's best allies in the war on pests. Each bat can eat between a quarter and half of its weight in insects every night; a single Little Brown Bat can eat more than 500 mosquitoes in an hour! If you are able to attract even a small colony of 20 or so bats to a bat house on your property, over 20,000 mosquitoes, or a smaller number of heavier insects like beetles, gnats, moths or flies could be eaten in your vicinity every warm summer night.

The main thing we can all do to help bats is simply not to use insecticides. Chemicals are very easily absorbed into the thin skin of bats' wings, so bats are extremely susceptible to pesticide poisoning. Since bats are the most important predators of night flying insects, every little bat helps.

Dr. Merlin Tuttle's book, *America's Neighborhood Bats*, is an excellent source of information on bats.

INTRODUCTION TO CREATIVE HOME EC

I hated "Home Ick" in Junior High School. This chapter is my revenge for the "Mother-Daughter" fashion show and the fake cinnamon rolls. They should have let me take wood shop!

Every year, $8.8 billion is spent in the U.S. on toxic cleaning products whose manufacturers spew thousands of tons of toxic waste into the air and water. The average American uses more than 40 pounds of these toxic products per year.

According to the U.S. Office of Technology Assessment, 15% of all toxic pollution in the wastewater stream comes from private homes.

MORE BAD NEWS

According to The National Center for Health Statistics, there has been an increase in respiratory cancers and respiratory diseases in homemakers over the past forty years. The increase was attributed to the use of toxic cleaning products, since homemakers tend to be less likely to smoke than the general population.

EVEN MORE BAD NEWS

Most poisonings occurring in the home are caused by cleaning products, and most of the victims are under the age of six.

THE GOOD NEWS

Your common kitchen ingredients and household appliances have uses that June Cleaver never dreamed of. All the equipment and ingredients you need for a clean, nontoxic home are probably already in your home; they were in your grandmother's home too.

A clean home is not something "to die for"!

ALTERNATIVE USES FOR KITCHEN INGREDIENTS

You need look no further than your kitchen for many nontoxic solutions. Baking soda, ammonia, miscellaneous condiments, vinegar, and even garlic can do the jobs of toxic products.

BICARBONATE OF SODA (AKA BAKING SODA)

- *Remedy Black spot and Powdery mildew* by spraying roses with a 5% solution of baking soda and water—3 teaspoons of baking soda per gallon of water—a recipe based on research done by R.K. Horst, professor of Plant Pathology at Cornell University.

- *Remove sink odors* by pouring baking soda and boiling water down the drain.

- *Deodorize a carpet* by sprinkling baking soda over it and vacuuming the soda up one hour later.

- *Replace cleanser* by using baking soda sprinkled on a damp sponge for kitchen or bathroom scouring chores.

- *Clean silver:* Fill an *aluminum* pan with a mixture of one teaspoon of baking soda and one teaspoon of salt per cup of hot water. Submerge your silver in the hot solution for a few minutes, rinse, and wipe with a soft, dry cloth. The aluminum acts as a magnet to attract the tarnish away from the silver. Very tarnished silver may have to be done several times. Strips of aluminum foil in a glass or steel pot filled with the hot solution will also work. If you have large silver pieces to clean, cover the bottom of your stoppered sink with a sheet of aluminum foil, and fill the sink with hot water. Pour in the salt and baking soda mixture, then let your candlesticks have a relaxing soak. Don't try to save the solution; when I tried it, the aluminum foil corroded.

- *Clean your coffee pot* by filling it with cold water and adding a teaspoon of baking soda. Bring to a boil. After a couple of minutes, pour out the water and rinse the pot out well with clean water.

AMMONIA

- *Evict groundhogs* from under your buildings by placing a bowl of cleaning ammonia in the area they are using. The fumes will drive them away almost immediately, and they won't return.

Low-Tech Wins Again!

Microbiologists Dean Cliver and Nese Ak at the University of Wisconsin at Madison, tested cutting boards to see whether plastic or wooden ones were more hygienic. They doused plastic and wooden cutting boards with raw chicken juice spiked with live bacteria broth, and discovered that the bacteria thrived for hours on the plastic cutting boards, even after the boards were washed in hot, soapy water. The same bacteria died out within three minutes on wooden cutting boards, even if the wooden boards were not washed! (Cliver and Ak are investigating the possibility that wood fibers dehydrate the bacteria and kill them.) Keep washing your cutting boards, plastic or not!

- *Repel Gophers* by placing ammonia-soaked sponges in their entrance holes.

CONDIMENTS

- *Remove pine pitch, tree sap, grease or tar* from your hands or your car with mayonnaise: rub mayonnaise on the sticky skin or car finish, let it sit a few minutes, then wipe it off.

- *Remove crayon marks from wooden furniture* with mayonnaise: rub mayonnaise on the marks, let sit for a minute or two, then wipe it off with a damp cloth.

- *Remove oil paint from your hands* by rubbing them with butter. Don't ruin a whole stick for this purpose: cut off a small piece to use for paint removal. (This would be the ideal use for rancid butter, but butter never lasts long enough at our house to go rancid.)

- *Remove ball point pen ink from carpeting* by covering the stain with salt and vacuuming the salt up as the stain is absorbed. Repeat the process until the stain is gone.

VINEGAR

- *Wash windows:* Mix equal parts white vinegar and water and spray from a bottle. Wipe the windows dry using crumpled newspaper to keep the windows from streaking.

- *Spray and Slay Slugs:* Fill spray bottles with a half and half solution of vinegar and water. Go into the garden at night with flashlights and spray the slugs with a "stream" setting. The vinegar causes the slugs to slime to death. If your children are slightly sadistic they may enjoy slug hunting.

- *Cure Fire blight*: This bacterial infection, which causes branches of trees to look black and burned, can be stopped by spraying the infected tree—especially the infected area—with a water and vinegar solution: 2 parts vinegar to 3 parts water. Spray again after two weeks.

- *Repel ants:* Wipe counters down every day with cider vinegar. If your castle has marble counters, instruct your servants to not wash the counters with vinegar: vinegar dissolves marble!

- *Kill head lice:* wrap the afflicted head in a vinegar soaked towel. (Do not remove head before doing this, it should remain attached to the body, no matter how angry you are at your child for bringing lice home!) Cover the wet towel with a dry towel and leave on overnight. The vinegar dissolves the lice and their eggs so they can be shampooed away the next day. Everyone in the household should be treated at the same time. All towels and bed linens should be washed with hot water, and all the furniture should be vacuumed.

- *Make a cleaning compound:* add one quarter cup of baking soda, one half cup of white vinegar, and one cup of clear ammonia to one gallon of hot water. It's good for cleaning floors, woodwork, and greasy stoves—and it kills mildew and doesn't need to be rinsed off!

- *Remove mildew:* spray it with vinegar water, then wipe the mildew right off!

- *Repel fleas and ticks*: add one tea-spoon vinegar to each quart of your pets' drinking water.

- *Clean tubs, sinks and toilet bowls* with full-strength white vinegar.

- *Clean out mineral deposits in copper teakettles* : boil one part vinegar and one part water in the kettle, let soak until cool, then pour out and rinse with clean water.

- *Prevent grease buildup on oven walls* by wiping the walls with vinegar on a damp cloth.

- *Use as a laundry softener*: just add one cup of white vinegar to the rinse cycle.

- *Prevent diaper rash*: first soak diapers in vinegar and water in the diaper pail, then add a cup of vinegar to the wash water. The vinegar helps kill off the bacteria that cause diaper rash.

- *Clean pet urine out of carpets*: combine three tablespoons white vinegar, one quart of warm water, and a drop of dish soap. Apply the solution gently to the vicinity of the "accident" with a rag. Blot dry with thick rags.

WARNING! NEVER MIX VINEGAR WITH CHLORINE BLEACH OR WITH CLEANSERS CONTAINING CHLORINE!

Combining these elements can cause emission of potentially fatal chlorine fumes. In fact, chlorine bleach and cleansers containing chlorine should never be mixed with anything other than water.

GARLIC

Garlic repels those vampires of the garden: the sucking insects. When you're done re- pelling for the day, the garlic (and on- ion) odor can be removed by washing your hands thoroughly with *cold* water and soap. (Hot water washes the odor *into* your skin).

- *Save your strawberries:* plant garlic amidst your straw- berry plants to repel insects.

- *Rescue your roses:* one clove of garlic planted near roses helps repel aphids and greenflies.

- *Fend off fungus:* prevent downy and powdery mildew and keep seedlings from damping off by boiling ten cloves of garlic in one quart of water for thirty minutes. Let cool to room temperature, strain, and use as a spray.

- *Protect your plants*: Make an insecticidal garlic spray. Sim- ply soak three ounces of finely minced garlic in two tea- spoons of *mineral* oil for 24 hours. Slowly add to a mixture of one pint of water and one quarter ounce of insecticidal soap. Stir thoroughly and strain into a glass jar for stor- age. Combine one to two tablespoons of this mixture with a pint of water and spray on insect infested plants. If plants' leaves are damaged, dilute more.

- *Rodale's All Purpose Spray:* Liquefy one garlic bulb and one small onion, add one teaspoon powdered cayenne pepper and mix with one quart of water. Let steep for one hour, strain through cheesecloth, then add one tablespoon liquid soap. Mix well and use.

Leave the soap out, and you can use this recipe to flavor your chili!

SOAPS, TOILETRIES, LAUNDRY AIDS, & DETERGENTS

The soaps, shampoos, and other toiletries we use affect the quality of the water that goes down drains and, eventually, into our waterways. They can also affect our own health more immediately, since some of what we put on our skin is absorbed into our systems. Read the labels of "beauty products" before you buy them. My motto is, unless there's a pressing medical reason, I don't put anything on my skin or that of my children that isn't safe to eat.

Many shampoos and other "beauty products" contain formaldehyde and other toxic substances. Formaldehyde may improve the beauty of embalmed corpses and dissected frogs, but I don't think it could really improve the looks of live human beings! Luckily, there are many brands of shampoos, hand lotions and other products which are made of safe ingredients; they can easily be found in health food stores and co-ops. Just read the labels!

PUT 'EM THROUGH THE WASH!

- *Kill lice* with coconut oil. To get rid of head lice, wet hair, apply a shampoo containing coconut oil, lather thoroughly, rinse. Repeat, but leave suds in hair, wrap head and hair in a towel, leave on for one half hour, remove towel and comb hair with a nit-comb. Wash hair again and rinse.

- *Knock down and kill wasps and bees* by spraying them with hair spray.

- *Battle mosquitoes* with Avon's Skin So Soft™ (A well-tested folk remedy used in Minnesota, land of 10,000 lakes and trillions of mosquitoes). Apparently, the fragrance molecules in Skin So Soft™ are exactly the right size to clog up mosquito antennae, so the mosquito's sense of smell stops working.

Whatever you use to ward off mosquitoes, avoid the pesticide DEET.™ The British medical journal, *Lancet*, published research which pointed out that slurred speech, staggering gait, agitation, tremors, convulsions, and death have all been documented consequences of DEET™ use. (Thanks anyway, I'll just scratch!)

- *Keep deer out of the yard:* A 1987-1988 study of deer repellants conducted at the Smithsonian's National Zoological Conservation and Research Center in Front Royal, Virginia, showed that one of the most effective repellants was Lifebuoy™ bar soap. Leave the soap in its wrapper, drill a hole in it, put a wire through the hole, and hang it in a tree. If you have a very severe deer problem, you may want to hang several bars in each tree.

- *Remove Eau de Skunk* by washing the odoriferous victim (usually a dog) as soon as possible in laundry soap—not detergent. Ivory Soap is good. Follow the wash with a vinegar and water rinse. (A dab or two of vanilla extract helps cover lingering odors until they go away.)

- *Kill rats and mice:* Leave an open box of powdered laundry starch where there are signs of rat and mouse activity, but out of reach of children and pets. The rodents eat the starch, and die of constipation.

- *Kill Ants*: Mix Borax™ or boric acid with sugar and put the compound in an area accessible to ants but inaccessible to children and pets. Block the ants' entrance holes with caulk or putty.

- *Kill cockroaches*: sprinkle Borax™ or boric acid in their runways, out of reach of pets and children. It works indefinitely.

- *Relieve cattle bloating* caused by overly rich food (bloat can kill a cow quickly): mix one tablespoon of a nonadditive, unscented detergent with one quart of water and pour the detergent water down the cow's throat. The detergent breaks up the surface tension of the gas bubbles in the cow's stomach so the gas can be belched out. (Cow belches, of course, add to global warming by putting more methane into the air; it's all the cows' fault.) Use the detergent cure only in an emergency! (I couldn't resist this one, even though I realize that some of you do not own cows.)

- *Keep grease off hands:* (This works great for auto mechanics.) Rub one or two tablespoons of liquid dish soap over your hands and arms *before* working on a car. Let the soap dry before you start to work. When you're ready to clean up, use more dish soap, and the grease will wash right off.

Soap Sprays

Soap sprays are highly effective at killing soft-bodied insects like aphids, scale, and whiteflies. Use the least-perfumed dish soap or liquid household soap you can find, or buy Safer's Insecticidal Soap™ (it's formulated so it doesn't make suds) and follow the procedure below.

1. Follow directions on the insecticidal soap label or use a one-and-a-half to two percent solution for most liquid household soaps. (For example, one teaspoon of Shaklee's Basic H™ per gallon of water or one tablespoon of Ivory Liquid™ per gallon of water.)

2. Use soft water or rainwater only.

3. Isopropyl (rubbing) alcohol added to insecticidal soap increases the soap's efficiency. The alcohol penetrates the insect's waxy protective covering. Use one half cup of alcohol per quart of water to dilute the insecticidal soap.

4. Spray in the evening to prevent the leaves from burning.

5. Use a high pressure spray.

6. Cover plants thoroughly, top to bottom and under leaves.

7. Repeat when necessary.

- To kill ants, brew concentrated mint tea and use it instead of water to dilute Safer's Insecticidal Soap™ to the proper dilution. Put the mixture in a spray bottle. It kills ants on contact and repels survivors.

Stop! Don't Throw that Away!

Some items we readily toss into the garbage because they've outlived their traditional usefulness can be used for tasks we often leave to chemicals. Try some of the following ideas as alternatives:

- A *rotten potato* makes a good *dog repellant*, and will probably repel bad dogs as well.

- *Hair of the Dog* : Save Fido's hair to use in the garden as a *raccoon repellant.*

- Don't wash that *stinky, sticky, stiff undershirt!* Not yet anyway. Hang it in your garden to *repel raccoons.* Replace it with a stinkier one frequently.

- Grind up *sunflower hulls* and drop them into the cracks of driveways or sidewalks to *prevent weeds* from germinating.

- If you want *to prevent weed grasses,* sprinkle *cornmeal* (preferably stale) over your plot of ground. The cornmeal inhibits germination of weed grasses, and its 10% nitrogen content fertilizes the soil at the same time. (Based on research by Nick Christians, professor of horticulture at Iowa State University.)

- Sprinkle dry *cornmeal* over your garden to *get rid of cutworms.* The cutworms eat the cornmeal but can't metabolize it, so it kills them.

- *Toilet paper tubes* can be used as collars to *prevent cutworms* from chewing plants off at ground-level. Put a tube one inch above ground and one inch below ground around young transplants.

- *Repel slugs and cutworms* with *crushed eggshells* strewn around plants. The pests don't like to crawl over the sharp broken eggshells. Eggshells are also a good source of calcium for the soil.

- *Keep slugs out* of your garden beds by sprinkling *wood ashes* around the perimeter of the garden. The barrier must be renewed after every rain.

- *Gnat and mosquito trap:* Put one cup of vinegar, one cup of sugar, and one banana peel in a clean gallon milk jug. Fill the jug with water and shake well. Hang the uncapped jug in a tree.

- *Wormless apples:* Put one banana peel, one cup of sugar, and one cup of vinegar in a clean one gallon milk jug. Add enough water to almost fill the jug, shake well, and hang the uncapped jug in your apple tree before the blossoms open. The

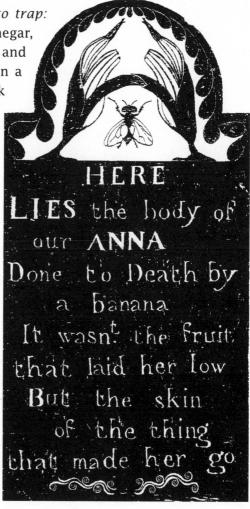

HERE LIES the body of our ANNA
Done to Death by a banana
It wasn't the fruit that laid her low
But the skin of the thing that made her go

apple codling moth is attracted, but bees aren't. Replace as needed.

- *Wormless Apples, part II*: Put one cup vinegar, one third cup molasses, one eighth teaspoon sweet pickle juice or ammonia, and one quart of water in a plastic gallon jug. Hang two uncapped jugs in each tree before blossoms open.

- Use *quack grass* to kill slugs. When it dies, this annual weed grass emits a gas poisonous to slugs. When you pull up your quack grass, throw the grass blades into your strawberry bed and leave the roots out in the sun to die. (Based on research by Roger Hagin of the Plant Protection Research Center in Ithaca, New York.)

- Ground-up *grapefruit rinds* can be scattered on the soil after you have planted your garden to *repel cats and dogs*.

- *Cucumber peelings* will *get rid of black ants*. Spread peels by ant trails in your house; the ants eat the peels and die!

- *Horseradish leaf tea kills fungus on fruit trees*. Pour four parts boiling water over one part horseradish leaves. Let tea cool, then strain it into a sprayer.

House Plants are Our Friends

Dr. Bill Wolverton, Senior Research Scientist at the National Space Technology Laboratories in Mississippi, found that common foliage plants can remove contaminants from the air in houses. He estimates that 15 to 20 plants would purify the air in the average energy efficient house.

- *Rhubarb leaves kill aphids.* Rhubarb leaves are highly poisonous. After you have made strawberry rhubarb pie with your rhubarb stems, boil one pound of the rhubarb leaves in one quart of water for 30 minutes, strain, then add a dash of liquid soap to make it stick. Spray it on aphids to kill them. Use rhubarb spray only on *ornamental plants.*

- *Tomato leaf tea kills aphids* and *corn earworms* (and attracts tiny, beneficial, Trichogramma wasps). Leave two cups of chopped tomato leaves in two cups of water overnight. Strain tea the next day and add two cups of water. Spray plants thoroughly.

Used Beverages

Coffee Break

Don't throw out that old, cold coffee. Pour it on your uninvited insect guests.

Dr. James A. Nathanson, a neurologist at the Harvard Medical School found that concentrated doses of caffeine killed insects within hours or days. He used powdered coffee and tea.

When exposed to caffeine, mosquito larvae get so uncoordinated they drown; tobacco budworms stop eating, develop tremors and die; and mealworms can't reproduce.

Coffee *grounds* are useful too:

- *Kill ants in lawns* by pouring one pound of coffee grounds in a quart of boiling water over the anthill. A very big anthill may require a larger amount of coffee and hot water.

- *Remove smoke smells from a car* by leaving shallow containers of fresh coffee grounds under the car seat.

- To *remove smoke smells from a couch:* sprinkle dry coffee grounds on the upholstery, wrap the entire couch in plastic, and seal it so it is airtight. Let it sit overnight or longer, then vacuum the coffee grounds up and shampoo the couch.

- *Remove freezer odors* by leaving a cup of coffee grounds in an open container in the freezer overnight. Remove the coffee grounds and repeat the next day if necessary.

MISCELLANEOUS BEVERAGES

- Use up your *soured skim milk* by spraying it on your plants to *kill plant viruses.* (Viruses often cause leaf mottling.)

- *Used tea leaves* sprinkled in your newly seeded vegetable garden will *repel radish and turnip maggots.*

- *Use stale beer* with a little sugar added to bait a *housefly trap.*

  The trap itself is made by cutting fly-sized entrance holes into a plastic beverage bottle. Cut the holes one inch apart, three inches above the bottom of the bottle, add an inch-and-a-half of beer, and cap the bottle.

  Flies fly upward toward the light after feeding, and can't find their way out. Leave the plastic label on the bottle to create more shade. (If you're fresh out of stale beer, bait the trap with decaying meat or fish placed in about an inch of water.)

- Sweet *wine* in the bottom of an open bottle can be used to *trap fruit flies.* Fruit flies are also attracted to a mixture of half grape jelly and half vinegar, left in the bottom of a bottle.

Butt Out, Pests!

Cigarette butts can be soaked in water to make an extremely toxic *bug spray*. Do not spray on crops just before harvest. Nicotine is a very powerful poison which can kill just about any living creature. (In 1990, according to the AMA, tobacco was the cause of an estimated 400,000 deaths and was the nation's leading killer.)

Tobacco top killer, AMA study shows

By Bob Geiger
News-Tribune Washington Bureau

WASHINGTON — Tobacco is the nation's No. 1 killer and its use led to an estimated 400,000 deaths in 1990, according to a review in this week's Journal of the American Medical Association.

The study, released Tuesday, found that tobacco use causes more deaths than alcohol, firearms, motor vehicles and illegal drugs combined. Tobacco use led to roughly 30 percent of all cancer deaths, 21 percent of heart disease deaths, and 19 percent of all deaths, the study estimated.

The conclusions are those of Dr. William H. Foege, health policy fellow at the Carter Presidential Center in Atlanta and a former director of the Centers for Disease Control. They based their study on a review of medical literature from 1977 to 1993.

Diet and lack of physical activity contributed to an estimated 300,000 deaths in 1990, the study said. Alcohol led to about deaths; infectious diseases by microbial agents other than AIDS, 90,000 deaths; toxic agents and contaminants, 60,000; firearms, 35,000; sexual behavior, 30,000; motor vehicles, 25,000; and illegal drugs, 20,000.

the study said.

Other factors such as and lack of access to are also important pact was more ure. the doct didn't estim aths due to ge-

rs pointed out that all e leading causes of ied in the study — to-and lack of exercise, — result from behaviors.

While the United States is expected to billion on

Citrus Solvent

This chapter ends with something no household should be without: citrus solvent. Grandma would have loved this stuff! Citrus solvent is a relatively new product on the market, marketed by different companies under different names. It is the concentrated oils from citrus peelings, and seems to be able to degrease just about everything from stoves to car engines. It can be used full strength for really tough jobs, (check first that it won't stain or dissolve the object you are trying to clean), or diluted for more delicate jobs, like cleaning walls or floors. I tried it out on the day-old bubble gum on a neighbor's chin, and the gum came right off, leaving the chin as good as new. It is also great for removing the adhesives which stay on new bathroom fixtures for years after the labels are removed.

I think citrus solvent shows great promise as an herbicide and pesticide as well: I tried it on slugs, and they died quite quickly. However, when I tested it out on a house plant to see whether it could be used as a pesticide for pests on plants, it melted my plant.

Give this product a try: for consumer and environmental safety, it beats all other solvents I know of.

CREATIVE USES FOR HOUSEHOLD EQUIPMENT

Organic pesticides are made of natural materials and biodegrade rapidly so they don't accumulate in the environment. However, they are still poisons, or they wouldn't kill "pests." The safest way to get rid of pests is to do it the old-fashioned way: squash 'em.

As we approach the twenty-first century, we modern citizens have acquired sophisticated household equipment that can be used to do things the old fashioned way. No, I am not talking about home bread-making machines; I refer to even more common equipment like central heating, vacuum cleaners, and glue.

My nine-year-old son came up with a novel pest control idea while we were at a barbecue last summer: he skewered a grasshopper, roasted it, and ate it. He roasted one for me and it wasn't bad, but I think some hot spices would have improved it.

Don't be too disgusted at the idea of insectivory: worldwide, it is much more common for people to eat insects than not to eat them. However, if you are going to barbecue an insect to eat, make sure that your neighbors haven't been using pesticides. So many insects are resistant to pesticides, that an insect may be flying around quite happily with a dose of pesticides in its body that could make you sick.

BARBEQUE

- *Safer, cleaner starts:* A piece of household equipment that every red-blooded barbequing family should own is a chimney starter for getting charcoal briquets going. A chimney starter is a metal cylinder with a handle. Crumpled newspaper is put in the bottom of the cylinder, and the briquets go on top of the paper. You light the paper, and in half an hour the briquets are ready to pour into the barbeque. It's a much cleaner, safer, and cheaper way to start the coals than using charcoal lighter. Many hardware stores carry these chimney starters, and they can also be mail-ordered.

- *Banish musty odors* from closed up cottages, closets, and refrigerators by leaving out an open pan of charcoal briquettes. The briquettes can still be used for barbequing after they have been used to soak up odors.

Bombs Away!

If used incorrectly, roach bombs blast more than just bugs. Play it safe and use less-volatile methods.

Birthplace of 'Streetcar' is no more

NEW ORLEANS — Where **Tennessee Williams'** creative fires once burned, a more literal fire has destroyed.

Six "roach bombs" caused an explosion Tuesday that injured two people and wrecked the French Quarter apartment where Williams wrote "A Streetcar Named Desire."

Flames from a water heater ignited the insecticide spray.

Cheron Brylski, who had just rented the third-floor apartment, had set off the aerosol cans of insecticide in the 8-by-10 kitchen Sunday. The recommended treatment — along with a warning to put out any open flames — is one can for a 20-by-30-foot room.

The blast blew out windows and the kitchen ceiling and buckled the apartment's floor and walls. It also blew the front door of the three-story building onto a passer-by. Brylski and the passer-by suffered cuts and bruises.

Williams lived in the apartment in 1946-47 while writing the play that won him the 1948 Pulitzer Prize for drama. He died in 1984.

Two More Good Reasons to Avoid Chemicals

Auto-Immune Disorders

Are your cells paranoid?

Auto-immune disorders such as rheumatoid arthritis can be induced in laboratory animals by exposing them to very small doses of chemicals which are considered nontoxic by themselves. In combination, these chemicals can overstimulate the immune system into an allergic overreaction in which the body attacks its own connective tissues. The body responds to real and imagined enemies in what has been called "cellular paranoia." The more chemicals that are loose in our environment, the more likely we are to get sick.

Varying Toxicity

"It can sometimes take a thousand or ten thousand times as high a dose to produce toxicity in one animal as in another. This difference is very important to consider when we are thinking about using toxicity data from animal experiments and applying them to human beings."

—Dr. Michael A. Kamrin, *Toxicology: A Primer*

Experimental hepatitis drug kills 5th volunteer

Associated Press

A fifth volunteer died Tuesday from an experimental drug touted as a miracle cure for hepatitis B, beyond medical rescue even as scientists unraveled the mystery of what

shown great promise for fighting the hepatitis B virus, which can cause deadly cirrhosis and liver cancer. When dogs passed toxicity tests unharmed, the Food and Drug Administration approved FIAU for human

recovering from an Aug. 4 transplant at Emory University Hospital in Atlanta.
Additionally, Hoofnagle fears other antiviral drugs such as the AIDS drugs AZT and ddI, which are known to be toxic, may at-

But FIAU didn't stop there. It also tricked sub-units of the body's cells called mitochondria, the all-important engines that energize the cells.
Mitochondria have their own DNA

VACUUM CLEANERS

- *Vacuum bugs out of your crops.* Plant eaters are slow and stay on the tops of the plants; predator insects stay out of the way. It is preferable to use a wet/dry shop vacuum for this so you don't get electrocuted if you vacuum up or stand in water.

  A huge commercial vacuum, called Bug Vac, is used very successfully in strawberry fields.

- *Remove houseflies, fruit flies and mosquitoes* from your home by vacuuming them up. Yellow jackets could also be vacuumed up with a wet/dry shop vacuum, but put several inches of hot soapy water in the bottom of the vacuum cannister first to make sure the insects don't emerge alive! Plug up the vacuum hose after vacuuming until you are sure there are no survivors.

- *Vacuum Whiteflies* out of your garden or greenhouse.

- *Suck up dandelion seed heads* to prevent dandelions from spreading. This technique works on thistle seeds too, though bear in mind that many small songbirds need thistle seeds to eat.

GLUE

- *Insecticidal glue spray:* Mix four fluid ounces (one half of an average-sized bottle) of white household glue (like Elmer's™) in one gallon of warm water. Spray the glue mixture on the twigs and leaves of infested fruit trees; soft-bodied bugs like aphids, red spider mites, scale and mealybugs will all be killed. When the glue is dry, it will flake off with the dead insects. Repeat treatment in seven to ten days if necessary.

- Remove a small splinter by putting a thin layer of white glue over the splinter. Let the glue dry, then peel it off. This works for wood and fiberglass slivers as well as for small thorns.

THE FURNACE:

A COLD AIR TREATMENT FOR MOTHS

If you live in a very cold climate, your heating system may be keeping moths alive in the winter. When the outside temperature is less than 0° Fahrenheit, take moth-infested furniture and clothing outside and leave it outside or in an unheated garage for a week. The pests will freeze to death.

GORY AND DISGUSTING

This chapter is my favorite. Please do not assume from this that I am a bloodthirsty monster. Those who object to the ideas contained within this chapter would do well to contemplate the alternatives. Is it really better to have a quick, "clean" kill due to poison, which can continue to kill and maim other creatures long after the target organism is dead? (Imagine a dopey poisoned rat being caught and eaten by your cat.) Or is it better to be more intimate with the creatures you're dealing with—to get your hands dirty, but leave your environment clean?

It is indeed better to use non-chemical pest control rather than synthetic poisons, but think hard before you meddle on a large scale. Even the organic insecticides like rotenone, pyrethrum, nicotine, sabadilla, and Bacillus thuringensis (B.t.), should only be used cautiously and in the evening. The organic pesticides break down safely, but can have unintended victims before they decompose. Just about everything except B.t. is toxic to honeybees, and B.t. is toxic to all caterpillars, not just pest species.

Even hand picking "pests" can have its drawbacks: I once squashed dozens of ugly spiky caterpillars which were defoliating my Dusty Miller plants. Later, when we looked up the caterpillars in a guide book, I discovered to my horror that I had massacred dozens of baby Painted Lady Butterflies! I bet E.B. White had lots of Painted Lady Butterflies on his farm in

Maine, where he described himself in *One Man's Meat* as: "…a man who hardly dares shoot a crow for fear of upsetting the fine adjustment in the world of birds and insects, predator and prey."

According to the Chaos Theory, which is revolutionizing science, it is possible that a butterfly waving its wings could affect the weather halfway around the world a month later.

Even archy the cockroach understood this when he quoted the spider: "curses on these here swatters/what kills off all the flies/ me and my poor daughters/unless we eats we dies."

On Borneo, insecticide spraying to eradicate malaria killed off more than mosquitoes. The Dyak people's villages were left catless almost overnight when their feline friends, whose principal food was cockroaches, ate poisoned roaches. Rodents quickly became so numerous and fierce that they began to attack children.

If you really want to be scared out of your wits, try reading the labels on garden pesticides and herbicides. It's illegal to use the stuff without reading the label, but almost no one who uses it ever does read the label...

Think of the following as pest control Charles Addams would have approved of.

OF SLUG BREAD AND BEHEADED THISTLES...

• Slug Bread

Pour three-and-a-half cups of lukewarm water into a large bowl, and add one cake of yeast (or one tablespoon of yeast). Let the yeast dissolve, then add one quarter cup of sugar, two teaspoons of salt, and four cups of flour. Mix well, and let it sit for a while as you find some empty plastic milk jugs with lids, and cut a few quarter sized holes about halfway up their sides. Pour an inch of the slug bread into the jugs. Then go out and bury the jugs so the holes are sitting just above ground level in your garden. The slugs are attracted to the smell of the fermenting dough, crawl in the convenient holes in the sides of the jug, and never get out alive! Empty the slug bread when it gets really disgusting, and pour in some fresh dough. Refrigerated dough will keep for weeks.

- **Sloshed Slugs**

  Pour a couple of inches of stale beer into the milk jug slug trap described above. The slugs will drown happy.

- **Shocked Slugs**

  Slugs will not cross a barrier strip of flexible copper three inches high buried one inch deep in the soil. The moist, slimy slugs get an electrical shock whenever they touch the copper!

- **Bursting Beetles**

  Dust plants with dry wheat bran or cornmeal early in the morning to control Colorado Potato Beetles. The beetles eat the bran, drink, and then burst when the bran expands.

- **Exploding Roaches**

  Mix one-half cup baking soda with one table-spoon powdered sugar. Put the mixture in roach areas, out of the reach of children and pets. Roaches eat the mixture and explode! This works on silverfish too.

Researchers in California have discovered that, in restaurants with regular pesticide spraying programs, cockroaches were five to ten times more tolerant of organophosphates and up to three hundred times more tolerant of carbamates than normal. Unfortunately, the human beings who work in the restaurants are still quite sensitive to these poisons.

Organophosphates are modified nerve gases which were discovered by accident as by-products of nerve gas research in Germany in the 1930s. Organophosphates are responsible for 80% of the pesticide-related hospitalizations in the U.S. every year.

Carbamates, a broad class of chemicals used as insecticides, fungicides, or herbicides, are less acutely toxic than organophosphates, but they have been shown to break down into highly carcinogenic compounds.

- **Garden-Hose-Caterpillar-Water Torture**

Apple codling moth larvae and aphids can be killed by directing a strong spray of water directly at the trunks of afflicted trees. Pay special attention to rough and loose bark.

- **Gophigure**

Gophers are repelled by fish heads placed in their burrows. And who wouldn't be? (From *Gardening Without Poisons*, by Beatrice Trum Hunter.)

- **Petrified Mice and Rats**

Mix one part plaster of Paris and one part flour with a little sugar and cocoa powder. The rodents eat the snack, drink a little water, and then get plastered! Place in an area inaccessible to children and pets.

• Boiled Ants

A single queen, lurking deep in her nest, perpetuates the whole colony. Your mission is to kill her and, in so doing, eradicate the nest. You are not allowed to use any chemicals to complete your task. What do you do?

Answer: Very quickly, in order to avoid swarming workers, shovel off the top layer of the anthill. Immediately pour boiling water into the nest. Run! Any surviving worker ants will die of old age in a week or so. If the colony is still alive in a week, try again.

• Fermented Insects

Handpick offending insects, crush them, and let them rot in a jar of water under the afflicted plants to repel others of their kind. (*The Bug Book* by Helen and John Philbrick.)

• Gummy Moles

Wrigley's Juicy Fruit™ gum is fatally attractive to moles. While wearing gloves to prevent human scent from getting on the gum, unwrap a stick and roll it into a cylinder. With a stick, poke holes four to six inches apart in the mole's run, and drop a gum cylinder into each hole. The moles love Juicy Fruit™—no other flavor will do—but it clogs up their intestines and they die. (Originally published in the *Newsletter of the Dawes Arboretum* in Cincinnati, Ohio.)

Before you try to kill your moles, remember that they are insectivorous and probably eat a lot of harmful insects in your soil. Try to learn to live with them. You can use a lawn-roller to flatten their tunnels in your lawn—they really aren't noticeable anywhere else.

Kids! Don't swallow that gum!

- **Beheaded Thistles**

Off with their heads!

If you cut the head off a thistle just as it starts to bloom, it will bleed to death.

BUG JUICE

You can scare off plant-eating insects with a batch of bug juice made from some of their own. But always wear rubber gloves when dealing with bug juice—a cloth or paper mask may not be a bad idea either. You are dealing with germ warfare here.

- Capture a cup or two of your least-favorite insect. Use only one species per batch—do not mix and match! If you can find insects that don't look healthy, pick them especially; their ground up carcasses may infect other insects with viruses.

- Place insects in a retired blender with two cups lukewarm water and liquefy. Strain the goo through cheesecloth or a fine sieve that is not used for food. Dilute one quarter cup bug juice with one or two cups of water.

- Spray afflicted plant on both sides of leaves, and along stems and runners. Repeat treatment after rain. Spray bug juice in the evening only, as sunlight may kill the insect viruses.

- Clearly-labeled leftover bug juice may be frozen to use later.

- Do not use the bug juice blender for food ever again!

  (Bug juice recipe from *Rodale's Garden Problem Solver; Vegetables, Fruits and Herbs* by Jeff Ball)

FUN FOR THE KIDDIES

Actually, this whole book is for children, so they can be born strong, healthy, and intelligent, and stay that way.

Children, because of their rapid growth rates and high rates of cell division, their immature immune systems, and their high respiration and metabolic rates, are more susceptible to chemical poisoning than adults are. Prenatal exposure to chemicals can cause a variety of devastating birth defects and cancers.

Organochlorines, such as DDT and dioxins, can mimic the hormone estrogen. Exposure to these chemicals, even long term exposure to small amounts of these chemicals, can cause adults to have reproductive problems and cancers of the reproductive system. Children exposed to these chemicals before birth can be born with birth defects affecting their reproductive systems. Prenatal exposure can also cause children to be born with a tendency to develop cancers of the reproductive system, in the same way that children of mothers who took the anti-nausea drug DES during pregnancy, are at extremely high risk for these types of cancers.

Researchers have also discovered that globally, male fertility levels are less than half of what they were fifty years ago. Cancer, sterility, and birth defects may be overly harsh ways of dealing with overpopulation.

Worldwide, poor people are the most likely to be poisoned by hazardous substances, since hazardous facilities are almost always located in poor neighborhoods. Sick or undernourished people are also less able to ward off the effects of exposure to dangerous chemicals. The factory explosion in Bhopal, India, which released toxic clouds of methyl isocyanate used in making pesticides, could never have happened in Palm Springs.

Migrant farm workers in the United States are exposed to higher levels of poisons than the rest of us can even imagine. Many of these farm workers are children.

The only truly safe level of chemical use for anyone who has children, wants children or lives near children, is zero! Since pesticides can travel over 1,000 miles in the atmosphere before coming back to earth, only those who live well over 1,000 miles from children should use the stuff. Read labels

Demand that your local stores carry nontoxic products

before you buy or use gardening, pest control or pet products. Many products are so commonplace that people don't even think about them. "Weed and Feed" lawn fertilizers often contain 2,4-D and flea collars and aerosol bug sprays can make humans and pets acutely ill.

Try to encourage organic farming by buying organic food whenever you can afford to- it costs more at the checkout counter, but consider the difference in price to be a donation toward improving the health of all of our children at home and abroad.

Toxins bombard us at home

About the last place Americans thought they'd find toxins was the comfort of their own homes. But growing evidence points to dozens of seemingly benign products found there that are daily churning out a stream of toxic fumes and chemicals.

By Kathy Boccella
Knight-Ridder Newspapers

PHILADELPHIA — When the environmental movement started more than two decades ago, most people associated toxic chemicals with soot-chugging smokestacks or sludge-filled dump sites. No one gave carpets a second thought.

Well, things have changed.

A growing body of evidence suggests that dozens of seemingly benign products found in and around the home, the living room rug included, are daily churning out their own stream of toxic fumes and chemicals.

From pesticides to particle board, tap water to bathroom deodorizers, adhesives to dry-cleaned clothes, recent studies suggest that many household products may collectively pose more risks to human health and the environment over time than industrial chemical waste.

Far from conclusive, the studies nonetheless add to concerns about the plethora of pollutants in the home and raise questions about the way we live.

"Thirty years ago when a lot of these products were introduced, people thought, gee, isn't

this terrific. ... Now we're paying the price," said Joanna Underwood, the president of Inform Inc., a New York-based environmental group that analyzed data that chemical companies submitted to federal and state governments for its Toxics Watch 1995.

A 522-page report by Inform that was released last month found that numerous commercial products released chemicals into the air and the water and that those chemicals remained there for long periods.

Please see Toxins, Page 7A

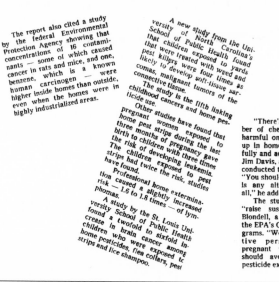

The report also cited a study by the federal Environmental Protection Agency showing that concentrations of 16 contaminants — some of which caused cancer in rats and mice, and one, benzene, which is a known human carcinogen — were higher inside homes than outside, even when the homes were in highly industrialized areas.

A new study from the University School of Public Health found that children exposed to yards that were treated with weed and pest killers were four times as likely to develop soft-tissue sarcomas, malignant tumors of the connective tissue.

The study is the fifth linking childhood cancers and home pesticide use.

Other studies have found that pregnant women exposed to home pest strips during the last three months of pregnancy gave birth to children with three times the risk of developing leukemia. The children exposed to pest strips had twice the risk, studies have found.

Professional home extermination caused a slightly increased risk — 1.6 to 1.8 times — of lymphomas.

A study by the St. Louis University School of Public Health found a twofold to sixfold increase in brain cancer among children who were exposed to home pesticides, flea collars, pest strips and lice shampoo.

"There's a tremendous number of chemicals that could be harmful on the market that end up in home. Many haven't been fully and adequately tested," said Jim Davis, an epidemiologist who conducted the brain cancer study. "You should not use them if there is any alternative available at all," he added.

The studies, while tentative "raise suspicions," said Jerry Blondell, a health statistician in the EPA's Office of Pesticide Programs. "We do advise that sensitive persons, particularly pregnant women and infants should avoid any unnecessary pesticide exposure."

FUN THINGS FOR KIDS TO DO

- **Make a volcano in a sink!**

To clear a clogged drain, pour one half cup of baking soda down the drain, then one cup white vinegar. The vinegar and baking soda will react chemically, releasing carbon dioxide which causes the vinegar to fizz. After the fizzing stops, have an adult pour a kettle full of boiling water down the drain.

- **Blast Bugs!**

Remove aphids and caterpillars from the trunks of your fruit trees with a strong spray from your garden hose.

- **Go Beach Bugging!**

Ladybugs are wonderful at controlling aphids. If you find a lot of ladybugs at the beach, carefully put them in a container with small air holes in it and bring them home to release in your garden. Ladybug larvae eat even more aphids than grown ladybugs do.

- **Bag Some Bugs!**

Catch insect pests to make bug juice with. Have a parent show you which insects to catch so you don't nab any helpful ones.

- **Spray Some Slimers!**

Go slug hunting at night with a flashlight and a spray bottle of vinegar and water (but try not to remind your mother that vinegar and water are very good for washing windows).

- **Build an Abode for a Toad!**

Create a toad house by knocking a chunk off the top of a medium sized clay flowerpot and turning the flowerpot upside-down. The missing chunk is the toad's door. Ask first to make sure you are choosing an unwanted flowerpot. Toads eat slugs, snails, and insects, so they are really useful in the garden.

- **Build A Bat Bungalow!**

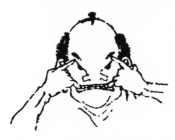

Help make a bat house. Bats are the best control of night-flying insects—each bat can eat several thousand mosquitoes per night! They also eat lots of beetles and moths. If there are enough bats in your garden, your apples might not have worms in them.

- **Give Your Dog the 'Tater Treatment!**

See what Fido thinks of a rotten potato. My dog hated the one I showed him. Put a rotten potato in your yard where dogs are creating problems. Do not use a rotten potato as a dog-repellant indoors.

- **Suck Up Some Bugs!**

Ask whether you can vacuum bugs out of the garden with a wet/dry shop vacuum. Wear hearing protectors whenever you suck up bugs—those big vacuums are loud!

- **Feeling Lousy?**

If you come home feeling "lousy," ask for the vinegar treatment to kill off the lice. Your brain will thank you for the nontoxic debugging.

Try some of these methods, then try inventing some of your own. Talk about it at the dinner table, especially if you have distinguished guests—your parents will love it! Your friends, relatives, and neighbors may also have their own methods: ask them for their formulas and start a disgusting recipe file!

The garden is a wonderful place to experiment, as long as you don't use toxic chemicals. Try ingredients from your kitchen and have fun!

My glass is run

BIBLIOGRAPHY

I have read a great many books on gardening and agriculture, and have found that many of the books which were written pre-World War II are more satisfying to read than some of the newer books. Before WW2, chemical agriculture was rare, and the agricultural pioneers who developed new techniques and wrote about them tended to be very interesting writers.

The following list includes the titles of some of my favorite gardening, agriculture, critter identification and home hints books. The particular copies I have chosen to list in this bibliography are the copies most likely to be in the collections of public libraries, so some books may be available in more recently published copies than those listed.

Ball, Jeff. *Rodale's Garden Problem Solver: Vegetables, Fruits and Herbs.* Emmaus, PA: Rodale Press, 1988.

Behler, John L. and F. Wayne King. *The Audubon Society Field Guide to North American Reptiles and Amphibians.* New York: Alfred A. Knopf, 1979.

(Reptiles and amphibians are our garden friends.)

Bradley, Fern M. and Barbara W.Ellis, eds. *Rodale's All-New Encyclopedia of Organic Gardening.* Emmaus, PA: Rodale Press, 1992.

Bradley, Fern M., ed. *Rodale's Chemical-Free Yard and Garden.* Emmaus, PA: Rodale Press, 1991.

Erickson, Jonathan. *Gardening for a Greener Planet*. Blue Ridge Summit, PA: Tab Books, 1992.

Hunter, Beatrice Trum. *Gardening Without Poisons*. Boston, MA: Houghton Mifflin Company, 1971.

Manning, Laurence. *The How and Why of Better Gardening*. New York: Van Nostrand Reinhold Company Inc., 1953.
(A classic old book of botany for gardeners.)

Milne, Lorus and Margery Milne. *The Audubon Society Field Guide to North American Insects and Spiders*. New York: Alfred A. Knopf, 1994.
(Before you squash, identify.)

Percivall, Julia and Pixie Burger. *Household Ecology*. Englewood Cliffs, N.J.: Prentice Hall, 1971.

Pfeiffer, Ehrenfried E. *Weeds and What They Tell*. Emmaus, PA: Bio-Dynamic Literature, Rodale Press, 1981.
(Diagnosing the condition of soils by identifying the weeds that are growing in them.)

Philbrick, Helen and John Philbrick. *The Bug Book*. Pownal, VT: Garden Way Publishing, 1974.

Proulx, Earl and Yankee Magazine Editors. *Yankee Home Hints, From Stains in the Carpet to Squirrels in the Attic: More than 1500 Ingenious Solutions for Everyday Household Problems*. Emmaus, PA: Rodale Press, 1993.

Riotte, Louise. *Carrots Love Tomatoes: Secrets of Companion Planting for Successful Gardening*. Pownal, VT: Garden Way Publishing, 1976.

Sabuco, John J. *The Best of the Hardiest*. Shelburne, VT: Good Earth Publishing, Ltd., 1985.
(All the plant-hardiness zone maps in this book have been redrawn after extensive field testing.)

Stein, Dan. *Dan's Practical Guide to Least Toxic Home Pest Control.* Eugene, OR: Hulogosi, 1991.

Stout, Ruth. *The No Work Garden Book.* Emmaus, PA: Rodale Press, 1971.
(Ruth Stout pioneered the technique of mulching gardens extremely heavily.)

Tuttle, Merlin. *America's Neighborhood Bats.* Austin, TX: University of Texas Press, 1988.
(Information on the bats most likely to be encountered in the U.S. Includes plans for building bat houses.)

U.S. Department of Agriculture Staff. *Common Weeds of the United States.* New York: Dover Publications, Inc., 1970.
(Never kill anything before you know what it is.)

Yepson, Roger B., ed. *Organic Plant Protection.* Emmaus, PA: Rodale Press, 1976.

Background Information

Balfour, Evelyn Bar. *The Living Soil.* Greenwich, CT: Devin-Adair Company, 1951.

Bailey, Liberty H. *Hortus Third: A Concise Dictionary of Plants Cultivated in the United States and Canada.* New York: The MacMillan Company, 1976.
(This is an immense book which is indispensable for the truly fanatic gardener. It is very expensive, however, and a search for a used copy is worthwhile.)

Boland, Maureen and Bridget Boland. *Old Wives' Lore for Gardeners.* New York: Farrar, Straus & Giroux, 1977.

Carroll, Lewis. *Alice's Adventures in Wonderland & Through the Looking Glass.* (available through various publishers).
(Nothing is what it seems in this book, as in life.)

Coccannouer, Joseph. *Weeds, Guardians of the Soil.* Greenwich, CT: Devin-Adair, 1950.

Darwin, Charles. *The Formation of Vegetable Mould Through the Action of Earthworms, With Observations on Their Habits.* New York: New York University Press, 1972.
(The great scientist spent many years studying the lowly earthworm, and discovered that it is one of the most important creatures on earth. This is a gem of a book, and one of my absolute favorites.)

Faulkner, Edward H. *Plowman's Folly & A Second Look.* Washington, DC: Conservation Classics Series, Island Press, 1987.
(This is indeed a conservation classic.)

Fukuoka, Masanobu. *The One-Straw Revolution.* Emmaus, PA: Rodale Press, 1978.
(A Japanese farmer waxes poetic about natural farming.)

Gleick, James. *Chaos: Making a New Science.* New York: Viking Penguin, 1988.
(A history of how scientists discovered that it is not possible to predict anything accurately within a complex system.)

Hill, John E. and James D. Smith. *Bats: A Natural History.* Austin, TX: University of Texas Press, 1984.

Howard, Albert. *An Agricultural Testament.* Oxford, England: Oxford University Press, 1979.
(A book by one of the original agricultural pioneers.)

Kamrin, Michael A. *Toxicology Primer.* Boca Raton, FL: Lewis Publishers, 1988.
(This is an extremely readable text about toxins. Even a layperson can understand it.)

Lappe, Marc. *Chemical Deception; The Toxic Threat to Health and the Environment.* San Francisco: Sierra Club, 1992.

Marquis, Don. *archy and mehitabel.* New York: Doubleday, 1950.

(archy the cockroach waxes poetic about life, man and insects.)

Osborn, Fairfield. *Our Plundered Planet.* Boston: Little, Brown, 1948.

(The author conducted experiments in soil building and no-plow farming.)

Sears, Paul B. *Deserts on the March.* Norman, OK: University of Oklahoma Press, 1967.

Schober, Wilfried. *The Lives of Bats.* New York: Arco Publishing, 1984.

Unger, Frederic W. *Epitaphs.* Philadelphia: The Penn Publishing Company, 1904.

(Nothing cheers me up like reading funny epitaphs.)

White, E.B. *One Man's Meat.* New York: HarperCollins, 1944.

(E.B. White wrote these essays from his farm on the coast of Maine about his relationship to the natural world.)

One Gardener's Guide to Periodical Literature

Magazines and journals can help keep you up to date on the latest discoveries. This book could not have been written at all without information from the following wonderful gardening publications:

Country Journal
P.O. Box 392
Mt. Morris, Ill. 61054

Countryside and Small Stock Journal
Countryside
W11564 Hwy. 64
Withee, WI. 54498

Harrowsmith Country Life
Telemedia Communications, U.S.A. Inc.
Ferry Road
Charlotte, VT. 05445

National Gardening
180 Flynn Avenue
Burlington,VT. 05401
(National Gardening is the National Gardening Association's Magazine.)

Organic Gardening
33 East Minor St.
Emmaus, PA. 18098-0099
(Organic Gardening is a Rodale magazine.)

North American Fruit Explorers' Pomona
Jill Vorbeck
Route 1 Box 94
Chapin, Ill. 62628

SOURCES FOR
ORGANIC NECESSITIES
OF HOME AND GARDEN LIFE

ORGANIC FERTILIZERS, PESTICIDES, AND SUPPLIES

Gardens Alive!
5100 Schenley Place
Lawrenceburg, IN 47025

Gardener's Supply Company
128 Intervale Road
Burlington, Vermont 05401-2850

HOUSEHOLD AND CLEANING SUPPLIES

Real Goods
966 Mazzoni St.
Ukiah, CA 95482-3471

The Vermont Country Store
P.O. Box 3000
Manchester Ctr., VT 05255-3000

INDEX

ATTENTION SCHOOLS
&
NON-PROFIT ORGANIZATIONS:

SELL THIS BOOK!

You can sell *Slug-Bread and Beheaded Thistles* for fundraising purposes and earn half of the retail price of each book you sell!

For more information on this golden opportunity, send a business-size, self-addressed stamped envelope (SASE) to:

Fund Raising
De la Terre Press
P.O. Box 16483
Duluth, Minnesota 55816